What texts say about you

What texts say about you

First published in Great Britain by Virgin Books Ltd
Virgin Books Ltd
Thames Wharf Studios
Rainville Road
London W6 9HA

A catalogue record of this book is available from the British Library.

ISBN-10 0753 5 11649
ISBN-13 9780753511640

The paper used in this book is a natural, recyclable product made from wood grown in sustainable forests. The manufacturing process conforms to the regulations of the country of origin.

Typeset by Phoenix Photosetting, Chatham, Kent
Printed and bound in Great Britain by Bookmarque Ltd, Croydon, Surrey

Contents

Text and
subtext

12tlk? Cul8a! ImOnTTrn! If you can read and understand these messages, then you were probably around in 2001, when the great text messaging revolution began. Of course, like jazz and rock and roll, fashion and sex, the young discovered it first, and made it their own. Originally designed for the phone service providers to communicate with the owner of the handset, the text service offered a limited number of characters, numbers and letters, to send messages, free at first, then at least cheaply, between handsets. This original service was also secret and secure, the perfect way for teenagers to communicate with one another, and no one any the wiser. The tell-tale click of the buttons might have indicated that they were playing games or idly tapping away their time, but in fact they were talking to one another and in a 'new' hybrid language of acronyms (some like ttfn and swalk, borrowed from an earlier generation's Second World War slang, though they would never believe it), abbreviations and emoticons borrowed from the other revolutionary new means of communication, the on-line chat room.

< Text and subtext >

Ruining the English Language

Soon text messaging evolved a language all its own, with a grammar that made it possible to send and receive instant, real-time messages, which only the techno bilingual could translate. Text language, like shorthand, is the spoken word translated into writing. To make sense of it you have to hear the words as if spoken aloud (ideally in an estuary English accent). First you drop as many vowels as possible and dispense with spaces between the words and conventional punctuation. Then, you use upper- and lower-case letters to indicate where a new word begins and to distinguish the sounds. Thus all new words, long sounds and double letters are shown by capital letters. Short sounds are shown with lower-case letters. Where possible the phonetic sound of a number replaces letters. So, Do you want to talk? will become 12Tlk, See you later CUL8a and so on. Emoticons, smiley faces and other figures made from punctuation marks and symbols were used both for fun, by creating silly pictures, and to indicate mood. Common words could be expressed in the same way every time they were used – w/ = with and w\ = without for example. Of course, the grown-ups were furious, and fierce debates raged on national radio and television about whether this new language was ruining the English language forever. We were given dire warnings that children would be unable to spell, as they would use this speedy language for all communications, including exam papers. Maybe a few did try to get away with this, and maybe a few had the answers sent to them, but on the whole all the fuss died down. Actually, text speak is a really useful shorthand for taking notes in class or lectures, and those who invented it and developed it showed an incredibly creative use of language and technology, which should have been encouraged, even creating poetry with wit and humour, but the purists couldn't see it.

Netiquette

It has to be said that within five years, some text abbreviations have become part of the English language and appear in both The Oxford English Dictionary and Webster's in the US. Even those guardians of etiquette, Emily Post in the US and Debretts in the UK have entries on the appropriate use of text! The abbreviations are frequently used in everyday life by advertisers to sell us products and to show how hip and cool they are. Just as jazz, soul and rock and roll were cleaned up and sanitised once they entered the mainstream, so the language of text was borrowed by the establishment, and its simple purity was lost. The grown-ups used the bits they could understand and ignored the rest, and anyone over ten who *was* cool and hip dropped it in favour of beautifully constructed sentences with conventional grammar and punctuation. Most people nowadays use only the simplest bits. It is about as cool as 'Dad dancing', if used too much by the over twenties.

You too can have the crazy frog
The manufacturers caught on, phones became more
sophisticated, the cheap option loophole was closed
up, and the secret and secure nature of the calls
was lost. But by then it was too late, texting was a
part of our lives. Many phone companies offer free
text time as an inducement to buy their packages.
Texting is still probably the quickest and cheapest
way to communicate from abroad. The technology
of mobile phones advanced so rapidly that they
can now sing, dance, tell jokes, send and receive
pictures and video clips, play a host of games,
send and receive emails, access the internet, and
download and play music. Videophones are now
quite commonplace and I fully expect my mobile
to make a cup of tea in the near future. I refuse to
discuss incredibly irritating ring tones. Blue tooth
technology has taken cell phones to a whole other
place. But text messaging *per se* has remained one
of the most popular functions of mobile phones.

< Text and subtext >

Moving on

In the early noughties, it was used to call the British Midland's faithful to prayer, organise a prison break in Singapore and free anally retentive men to express their emotions to women they hardly knew. More importantly, it began to be used by the clubbing generation to tell one another where they were going and to tell anxious parents that their children had arrived safely at their destinations. Texting has become such a part of our mainstream lives that we will soon be able to exercise our democratic franchise and vote for our government, in the same way that we vote to evict the latest wannabe celebrities from reality TV shows. Text is here to stay, even if the language that started it all has become a little passé.

< What texts say about you >

I know what you are going to say
It is fun to note though that the predictive text
now incorporated into our handsets, designed
to second-guess what it is we want to say, has
generated its own form of nonsense. Heaven knows
where it originates, but obviously somewhere in
Scandinavia, as it sometimes makes interesting
Nordic decisions about the word it thinks we want
and substitutes something truly strange.

Youth being young have adopted some of its
substitutions into their vernacular and so the
wheel goes on turning. We send literally millions
of text messages a day, making plans, chatting in
idle moments, sending and receiving information.
When we are not shouting loudly in the street or
on the train– like children who close their eyes
and imagine no-one can see them, we seem to
think that other people can't hear the details of
the hot sex we enjoyed last night or the row we
have had with our boss and just what he can do
with his ******* job – we are sending private and
secret messages by text. I can't help thinking that
those texts have become increasingly prosaic and
mundane as our conventional conversations have
become more outrageous.

So how do you use the text function on our
mobiles and what do the messages you send and
receive say about you. Now might be a good time to

take a wry look at the words bouncing around in the ether and off the satellites and into our brains. The names have been changed to protect the guilty! You know who you are.

I new
message

I predict
a riot

< What texts say about you >

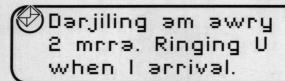

Darjiling am awry 2 mrra. Ringing U when I arrival.

(Darling I am away tomorrow. I will phone you when I arrive.)

You are almost certainly over 40, and you have just updated your phone. You are female and you do not read instructions. You may have incipient arthritis in your thumbs and you have never encountered predictive text before. You are charmingly eccentric. This message will probably be followed by several others apologising for your ineptitude.

SrE, SrE, my phone keeps sending messages before I'm ...

You are also over 40, and the whizzy new mobile you got for Christmas has tiny buttons, placed very close together and you keep pushing the wrong one. Grow your fingernails and use them to tap. Make an appointment for an eye test; reading glasses may be in order.

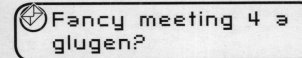 Fancy meeting 4 a glugen?

Would you care to have a beer? You have encountered one of the words, which your phone has decided should stand instead of beer. Make sure that your mates understand this or there could be confusion leading to shunning and withdrawing of plans for convivial nights in the bar.

Love is in
the air

Will you marry me?

If you are the receiver, it depends how you feel. Only you can know whether this is a person too mean to invest in the traditional, expensive, candlelit, romantic dinner for two, hot air balloon trip, or moonlit Bali beach vacation usually associated with marriage proposals. Perhaps he is too proud of his trousers to go down on his knees? On the other hand he may be incredibly romantic and knows what a huge buzz you will get out of opening this text on the bus or in the office? You must decide. I hope it's the latter.

< Love is in the air >

Can't wait 42NIt
Can U?
ILuvUIIkUIuvME

Either this message represents the very early stages of a very hot relationship or you are fishing to see how he or she feels about you. If the former, then great, have a wonderful life. If the latter, then don't. If you can't ask him or her straight out to tell you how he or she feels or can't tell from his or her manner when you are together then you are wasting your time. If you are female, yes, I know men find it easier to say 'I love you' in a text, but let him do so in his own time. People who fish for compliments get the old pram more often than the leaping salmon! If you are male, put her out of her misery, please.

IMSOHoTURHoTCUL8R.
TTFNLOLXXX
I'm so hot, you are
hot, see you later,
ta,ta for now, lots
of love

You could be under 10 or over 50, either way you have only just discovered txt spk and you are lovin' it! Just remember that it only works if the person you are texting understands what you are saying. If in doubt, spell it out.

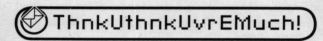 ThnkUthnkUvrEMuch!

You are dating an Elvis impersonator.

< Love is in the air >

I just realised I luv u!

You are probably male, over 40 and have just returned to the 'dating' world. Add to that a pinch of shyness and a whisker of the cowardly lion. I mean, when in the 80s did you announce in abbreviated form that you loved someone! Pick up the phone, send roses, take the lass to dinner. Also consider if this is really a potentially deep and meaningful relationship before you send it, or just an exciting new adventure of lust and romance.

< What texts say about you >

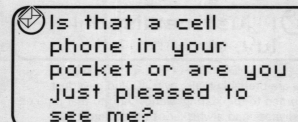

Is that a cell phone in your pocket or are you just pleased to see me?

Flirty, thirty-something or even forty, fifty or sixty-something, this is fusion messaging. You are either old enough or sophisticated enough to know the classic Mae West line, or young and cool enough to make it your own. It is to be hoped that the recipient is worth it. If the response is, 'No actually, and I fail to see how you can see what I have in my pockets from that distance and if you could, it would probably be my train spotter's handbook that I carry everywhere', or anything similar, give up and find someone who appreciates you.

< Love is in the air >

 Fluffy, wuffy
bunnywunny
luvs ickle darling
mousie wousie.
Snuffle snuffle.

If you sent this, you better be sure of the recipient's
feelings. Unless he or she is extremely like-minded,
this sort of mush is a real turn off. You should really
save this sort of talk for the privacy of your room
perhaps using glove puppets or your collection of
soft toys to act the parts of the participants.

< What texts say about you >

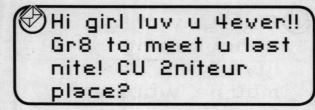

Hi girl luv u 4ever!! Gr8 to meet u last nite! CU 2niteur place?

You are an alley cat that confuses lust with love. Better to take an honest approach such as: I'm in it for the sex, how about you?

Cn't w8 2 get u alone, BIG Boy!

You are a fun-loving texter of any age. But this may be an indiscreet message if sent to a business mobile or someone with another partner.

< Love is in the air >

Ribbed or chocolate? 3 or 6?

If the sender is male he is indicating prowess and sense of fun or revealing a sense of responsibility for ensuring it a safe encounter. If female she is indicating availability and an adventurous spirit, but also taking control of your own destiny. If you don't understand the message, it is probably best not to enquire too deeply.

< What texts say about you >

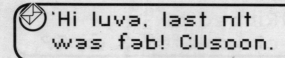

'Hi luva, last nlt was fab! CUsoon.

'Yes wasn't I?'

Either your 'luva' has the wrong end of the stick or you do. She clearly thinks a relationship is going on and you are majoring on your own performance. This is also an unkind but effective response if you want to end a brief affair. Send to those you care about and you show a lack of sensitivity. Pick up the phone and talk to them.

The end of
the affair

< What texts say about you >

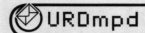 URDmpd

(You are dumped)

If you are the sender: you are under 25 (probably under 10) and could be male or female. You are not brave enough to talk to a rejected lover face-to-face and you have a limited command of the language. You watch too much television, especially youth soaps in which people are constantly dumping one another by text message.

If you are the receiver: don't fret, find someone who appreciates you and has a little more finesse.

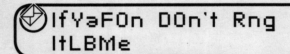 IfYaFOn DOn't Rng ItLBMe

(If your phone don't ring it will be me)

You are being dumped by a fan of bad Country and Western. Probably just as well, there are plenty more line dancers in the barn if that is your thing.

< The end of the affair >

IflSedUHdABUtiflBoD WldUHIdItAgnstMe?

(If I said you had a beautiful body would you hold it against me?)

If you are the sender: you are one of the plenty more line dancers in the barn. You are also hoping that using txt speak will cover up the fact that this is one of the oldest chat up lines in the book.

    If you are the receiver: you have been warned.

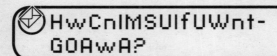

HwCnIMSUlfUWnt-GOAwA?

(How can I miss you if you won't go away?)

If you are the receiver: see, I told you! You are being dumped again by another Country and Western fan. Move on little missy. Time to try punk!

< What texts say about you >

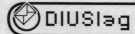

DIUSlag

(Go away you person of ill repute)

Sorry, punk was not such a good idea, Move away from musical genre altogether. 'Find a boy, settle down, if you want to you can marry, look at me, I am old but I'm happy!' Well more into pop and easy listening then.

Hi J. Sorry that I didn't call. I have been away on government work, knitting in Gaglestan and communication was very limited. Sadly, I won't be back in the country for another ten years, so I will quite understand if you want to date other people. Thanks for the good times. There is no longer any

< What texts say about you >

need to send me the same text ten times a day.

If you are the sender: I think you are trying to be kind. It might be easier to change your number, name, and dye your hair. A beard and moustache might also help.

If you are the receiver: he's just not that into you.

< The end of the affair >

 Sorry I haven't replied to your ten messages a day. I've run out of call credit/my battery has run low/I left my mobile at home/my mobile was stolen.

He's just not that into you.

 GrrrArgh

It's the end! One Buffy the Vampire slayer fan to another.

Wish you were here

< What texts say about you >

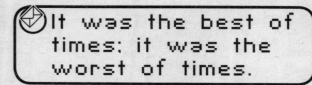

It was the best of times; it was the worst of times.

You are a literary S&M fan who is at a convention of like-minded friends in Finland and you wish your like-minded friends at home to know that you are having a good time, in your own special way.

< Wish you were here >

Dear Friends in the caravan club. There are so many of you that G and I decided to send the same text postcard to you all as I know that you will all be longing to hear about the fabulous holiday we are having touring the motorway service stations of Eastern Europe. As you will see from the video slides that you

< What texts say about you >

will be receiving
shortly (these
are the best ten
of the 4250 we
have taken), there
is a tremendous
variation in the
standard of
facilities available
and in the quality
of a nice a cup
of tea and a
biscuit. Those of
you who know
the correct
colour for a
decent cuppa
may be shocked
by the slides.
Nevertheless,

< Wish you were here >

we are having
a great time as
the indifferent
weather doesn't
interfere with
our enjoyment
of the off road
parking. G has
gone reluctantly
to do a little
essential shopping
and to light a
candle in the 12th
Century cathedral
this morning, so
I thought I would
write to you
whilst I have a
free moment. We
will be pleased

< What texts say about you >

to see you all
at number 26 on
our return for
a glass of wine
and a cheese
and pineapple on
a stick. I know
you will want to
share the rest of
our holiday slides.
Fond good wishes
P

This person is either far past the post of post-ironic irony or someone to avoid like the plague, and this message is a blatant abuse of text messaging.

Poor G has obviously run off with someone who will show her a good time and is unlikely to return any time soon. Still, there might be a book in the comparative pictures of cups of tea, download to your computer.

< Wish you were here >

Hey, M8 Get yerself over here, booze cheap, great fry ups, birds gorgeous, pulling every night, saved I4U clubbing fantastic! Take a look at the pics of the birds on the beach. The one on the left is yours says her name is Pinot Grigio. Whhay! Toddy

You are under 25 (I hope!) and one of the millions of young adults who go abroad for sun, sex, booze and clubbing. If you received this, I doubt that 'Pinot' will still be free by the time you get a Flycheap flight to sunnier climes. Consider the Norfolk broads.

< What texts say about you >

Hi J, Remember me? Is everything OK, something must be wrong with my phone; I can't believe that you haven't been in touch since you got home. I still think about that great night on the beach, and how cool U R. My mate didn't believe me when I told her how much in love we are. When can I come and

< Wish you were here >

CU? Have you told your mum and dad about us yet?
My dad and my 3 brothers will bring me down to yours as soon as they get back from the Gulf. luvUBabe Pinot

Oh dear, you took that cheap flight didn't you? It is a mistake to promise a girl that you love her when you have no intention of seeing her once you get home. Pinot seems to have taken you very seriously and I suspect the male members of her family will feel the same way. Consider witness protection.

I'm on
the train

< What texts say about you >

I am on the train ETA 19.00hrs. Have dinner ready. Be at the third rail in the fence. Keep the car engine running. I don't expect to have to wait for you. Await further instructions.

You are a control freak who expects everyone to drop what they are doing to be at your beck and call. Try, 'Looking forward to seeing you, don't worry about cooking, we're going out, my treat!' That is if you want to change your life and those of the people around you immeasurably.

< I'm on the train >

 'Hi how is ur day going? Hope ur important meeting went well'

You respond ....not

You have a supportive colleague and you are so busy and important (read cool) that you do not respond. Create a template that reads 'Thx 4 txt all ok, will ring when can'.

It takes no time to respond if you are organised and at the very least will win you friends and influence people!

Deal fell thru, tell the boss. Am in quiet zone so do not ring.

If you are the sender, you are a survivor and probably a dab hand at PowerPoint. You have successfully made someone else the 'messenger' of bad news so he or she can be shot in your stead. If you were really clever, it was a rival for your boss's affection.

If you received this, forward it, just as it is, to your boss, or pretend you never got it. Watch your back in the office.

< I'm on the train >

Her to Him
You could have made the effort to listen to me last night.
Him to Her
What are you talking about? You weren't speaking to me.
Her to Him
Of course I wasn't speaking to you because you never listen to what I say, so you didn't even realise that I was trying to talk

< What texts say about you >

to you.
Him to Her
I was tired. I didn't
realise you were
having one of your
moods. What is it
this time?
I told you I'm
not ready for
marriage.
Her to Him
Who said anything
about marriage?
I wouldn't marry
you if you were
the last man on
earth.
Him to Her
That's okay then

< I'm on the train >

because I'm not
going to ask you.
Her to Him
I don't want you
to ask me, if I
wanted to marry
you, I would ask
you.
I'm not even sure
I want to see you
any more.
Why don't you
move your stuff
out of my place?
Him to Her
You don't mean
that?
Her to Him
Yes I do, I'm sick

< What texts say about you >

of the silences
and the rows.
Him to Her
Okay, I'll go if that
is what you really
want.
Her to Him
So I mean that
little to you.
Him to Her
No, of course not,
you know I love
you.
Her to him
Really?
Him to Her
Really, I can't live
without you.
Her to Him

< I'm on the train >

I love you too
babe.
Him to Her
Hurry home. I can't
wait to see you
tonight.

This couple have loads of free message time as
they change their service provider every three
months. They are in their mid-thirties and have
almost everything they want, but are both getting a
bit bored. They have replaced normal conversation
with text rows on the train, and though it doesn't
look promising in relationship terms, they both get
what they want. He does love her and doesn't want
to move out. She wants him to tell her how much
he loves her. Incidentally, she does want to marry
him. But as long as they never lose their phones,
they will be able to rescue this relationship from
the trash with each new day and enjoy making up
every night.

< What texts say about you >

The owl of
Minerva flies at
dusk over the
byre of destiny.

Okay, you are a spy aren't you? Either that or a fan of thrillers of the 1940s.

Only you, and the voices in your head, know what this means, but I hope that the recipient gets the message and meets you under the clock at Waterloo station at 5 o'clock, wearing a red rose in his buttonhole and carrying a rolled copy of *The Times*.

Every success with your mission.

I new message

What the stars might say

< What texts say about you >

 Scream, scream, moan, moan, biting hard on a leather strap, digging my nails into your hand. This will be our only child.

This could easily be a text from Katie to Tom during labour. Forbidden to scream, 24 hours of free text time, seemed like a good deal.

I'm up a tree!
Keith to Mick

I may not be available for the world tour.

I new message

Poetry in
motion

< What texts say about you >

Stndn @The Bus
Stp in The Ran
ULOkAwA$I
CnOnlEFElThePAn
IfUWldOnlESmlllSmll
@ ME
I CldLrn2Hop-
ThtRTroLuvCldB

(Standing at the bus stop in the rain,
You look away and I can only feel the pain
If you would only smile one smile at me
I could learn to hope that our true love could be)

You are very young aren't you? It is difficult to
make txtspk poetry scan, but your heart is in the
right place. Perhaps though, if you have his or her
mobile number, you know him or her well enough to
risk smiling first. Just a thought!

< Poetry in motion >

◈ MLuvIsLIkaRdRdROs

This is clearly a love message from a Scotsman, just read it exactly as written, with a Scots accent and with apologies to Robert Burns, it will be perfectly clear. Whether you respond or not to this message depends on how you feel about Scotsmen in general and this one in particular.

◈ ThundrbL$LitnVe- ReVeRE Frltn

I'm afraid of the thunder and lightning.
   From one Queen Fan to another.

< What texts say about you >

TiaYeLoRiBnRownd TheOlOkTrE

Clearly this message is from a middle-aged Tony Christie fan enjoying the singer's current revival and asking whether the girl or more probably middle-aged woman to whom he has been unfaithful will forgive him by first finding an old oak tree and then tying a yellow ribbon around it to indicate that she is still prepared to go on seeing him. If you receive this and even for one moment think of doing it, I suggest that you consider therapy.

Bad News
Texter

< What texts say about you >

> ## ✉ Sorry luv can't c u, wife's bak!

If you are the sender, you should probably be more discreet, unless you want your affair to be discovered. The fact that you are concerned about your wife finding out shows you are not really ready to throw your marriage away and hurt her. Where do you think those words go when you delete them? If you are the recipient, well the same applies really, except that you might want to ask yourself what you are doing with a chap who is both emotionally and actually unavailable. Text the cute guy at the office instead and don't spend your time waiting for this guy to be free.

< Bad News Texter >

> ✉ Bad news your cat
> was hit by a car.

You are pretty insensitive – the recipient could have
a heart attack or run into a tree. Sad news should
be broken gently and with compassion, preferably
with face-to-face support. A better approach is to
ask the party to ring you when they are free. When
they do contact you make sure they are not alone!

< What texts say about you >

Your dinner is in the dog

Your partner or your personal cook is seriously displeased with you and has left you for someone more considerate or punctual. The dog is the main beneficiary, always assuming that either the chef or partner is a good cook. This message is even more disturbing if you don't own a dog, are single and do not employ a chef. It could be that it has been sent in error, in which case, carry on. If someone cooks for you, but you cannot imagine what you might have done to deserve such a punishment, consider that it might be fate, diverting the message to you as an early warning of what could happen to you if you don't mend your ways. Pity the poor fool who missed this message and will go hungry tonight.

< Bad News Texter >

You're fired

Although you have been with the firm for ten years
and no-one has ever complained about your terrific
work, and although we all love you and value you,
unfortunately business has been bad recently and
because you have been here so long you are one
of our more expensive employees, so we can save
a little and keep the single mother in accounts on
instead. Take your time, we'll have a great leaving
party for you, and I am sorry to break the news to
you in this crass fashion but I am a moral coward
and have just found your mobile number, and
this saves embarrassment all round. Don't take it
personally, it's just business, and we will of course
give you a great reference.

Have a nice life!

If you are the sender, shame on you.

Mini Quiz

< What texts say about you >

How many texts do you send a day?

A Over 30
B 10–30
C 5–10
D 0–5

How many of your text messages are to friends and family?

A Over 75%
B 40%
C 25%
D 10%

How often do you have text sex?

A Every day
B Twice a Week
C Once a Month
D Never or Almost Never

Do you like to use emoticons?

A Yes love them – ☺☺☹
B Yes when I am writing to my friends and luv
C Occasionally to let someone know how I feel
D Naff, naff, naff and naff again!

< Mini Quiz >

How often do you text your true love?

A Every morning, lunchtime and evening
B Every morning and evening
C. Once a day
D Only when the mood strikes

How often do you vote for television surveys via text?

A Twice a week
B Once a fortnight
C Once a month
D Who votes for those stupid programmes???

Do you continually send texts to people who do not respond?

A Yes
B No
C Sometimes
D Absolutely Never

If someone frequently texts you do you respond to all of them?

A Always!!
B Usually
C Only if a response is required
D No, they are a bl**dy nuisance

How often do you send round-robin texts?

A Every day
B Twice a Week
C Once a Month
D Never or Almost Never

Have you ever written or sent a text poem?

A Often, both romantic and funny – 'Roses r red' & 'There was a girl from Nantucket'
B Regularly to my luv
C 4 special days – Valentine's day
D Never or Almost Never

Do you send holiday greeting text to friends and family.

A Yes instead of a card
B Yes if the card is going to be late
C Occasionally when I remember
D Never or Almost Never

What percentage of your texts are business related? This would include paying the London congestion charge, setting up meetings, advising of changes in schedule, quick updates etc.

A 0–10%
B 10–25%
C 25–50%
D 40% plus

< Mini Quiz >

On average how many info-texts do you send a day (e.g. arriving late, please pick up a loaf of bread, see you at the bar)?

A 0–3
B 3–10
C 10–25
D Over 25

What percentage of your texts are social (finding out how a friend is, sending congratulations or giving a message of support or sympathy?)

A Over 75%
B 40–75%
C 25–40%
D Less than 25%

Mostly As
My, you are busy aren't you? Or not… How do you find time to work or eat or sleep or have any kind of real life? Perhaps you are a teen, though I assume you do work, or else how do you afford all these texts. You are a real chatterbox and potentially a bit of nuisance. Cut back a bit, why don't you? Have some real conversations. Ask a friend out for a drink and a chat, and leave the phone at home. Texting all those TV programmes just makes money for the phone company.

< What texts say about you >

Mostly Bs

I would not be surprised to hear that you have a huge circle of friends and are very good at staying in the centre of your busy social whirl. You obviously enjoy writing texts more than you enjoy having face-to-face conversations. Perhaps it is because you can express that sexy streak by text. You may also be a tad overemotional.

Keep an eye on your text rate, if it goes up at all, consider a text amnesty.

Mostly Cs

You seem to be pretty well in control of your life and of your texting digits. You seem to have a sensible balance between texting for fun and to swap news and information. You are quite careful not to commit yourself on screen, very sensible, but perhaps a little too cool. Some of those to whom you text might think you are even lukewarm.

Mostly Ds

Oh dear, you really haven't come to terms with the text function on your phone have you? Or perhaps you are so afraid to communicate that you keep it strictly for urgent information messages on a need to know basis.

I would guess that you also keep your phone switched off, unless you are expecting an important call or want to make one yourself. It isn't just for emergencies you know, it can also be for fun. You might need a little more of that in your life. Oh and this book was probably a present.